Joey

Good morning, Joey. How are you?
Here's some water and some seeds for you.

Tweet-tweet!

I like this swing.

I like this ladder.

Joey is a happy bird. His house is a cage.

seeds   a ladder

1

One day Joey's cage is dirty. Mary opens his cage. Joey flies out and stands on Mary's shoulder.

No, Joey! No!

Mary is cleaning Joey's cage. Joey flies to the window. He can see some brown birds in the tree outside. The birds are singing.

opens

flies out

stands

outside

Mary is hot. She opens the window.

Oh! Good! I can go out. I can play with the brown birds.

Oh, no! Joey!

The window is open. Joey is flying out through the window.

through

Puzzles

1. Choose the right words.

cleaning

singing

flying

a) Mary is _singing_

b) The brown birds are _flying_.

c) Joey is _cleaning_ his wing.

2. Look at the pictures. Write the right words.

Joey and the brown birds are talking.

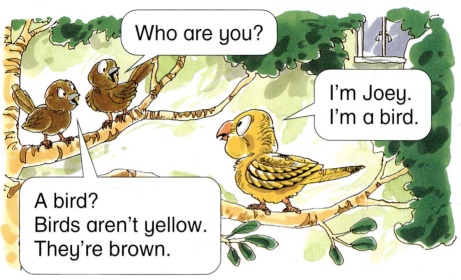

Who are you?

I'm Joey.
I'm a bird.

A bird?
Birds aren't yellow.
They're brown.

Look! I can jump.

What's that?

Yes!

Yes. He's a bird.
A yellow bird!

It's a nest. It's our house.

talking

a nest

Now the brown birds and Joey are on the ground.
The brown birds are eating.

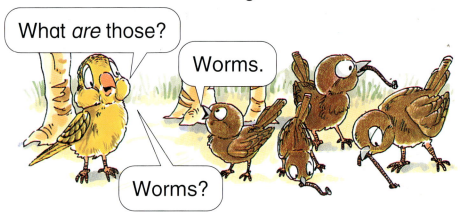

Joey is hungry. He can see a worm near the tree.

worms

The brown birds are flying.

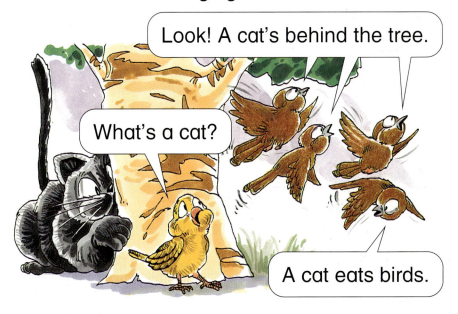

Joey looks at the cat. The cat looks at Joey.
The cat is hungry.

 **Puzzles**

1. What do they eat? Join the pictures.

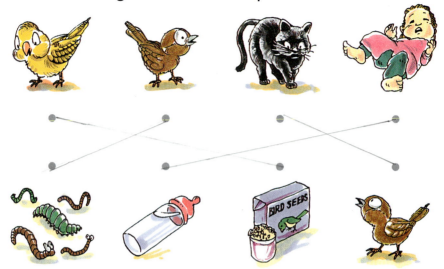

2. Look at the pictures. Write the right sentences.

   What's that?   Who are you?

a) who are you

I'm a worm.

b) what's that

It's a nest.

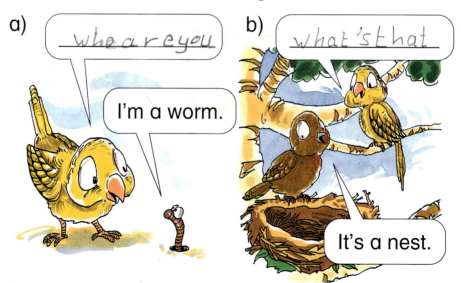

Joey flies up to the tree. The cat jumps.
The cat is hungry.

Help! I don't like cats.

Joey is afraid. He is at the top of the tree.
The brown birds are in the tree, too. The cat
is near the tree. The cat is looking at Joey.

Now the sun is behind the clouds. It is windy. It is raining. The cat is running. Joey is wet.

raining

Now the sun comes out again. It is shining.
Joey is dry.

Oh, it's sunny and warm.
What's that?

It's a rainbow.

It's super!

Joey is happy. He is flying. The brown birds are
flying, too.

Puzzles

Look at the pictures. Write the right words.

shining	raining	sunny	warm	cold
singing	behind	clouds	near	wet
running	under	at the top of		

a) A bird is _at t het of_ a tree. It is _singing_ Some

children are playing _under_ the tree. A cat is

near the children. The cat is _runing._

A dog is running _behind_ the cat. The sun is

shining. It is _warm_ and _sunny._

b) Now the sun is behind the _clouds_ It is

raining The cat, the dog, the bird and the

children are _cold_ and _wet_ .

12

Joey is flying above some flowers.

What are these?

They're flowers.

Smell them.

They're nice.

Hello, butterfly.
Your wings are beautiful!

What *are* those?

They're butterflies.

Oh, thank you.
I like your feathers.

butterflies

feathers

Joey is tired. He stands on a flower.

a beehive

Puzzles

1. Find these words in the word square.

bee

beehive

wings

butterfly

feathers

flowers

B	U	T	T	E	R	F	L	Y
E	P	S	H	O	U	L	D	O
E	U	B	O	A	I	O	Z	U
H	F	E	T	U	I	W	Q	R
I	F	E	A	T	H	E	R	S
V	E	R	Y	E	A	R	U	I
E	O	W	I	N	G	S	N	X

2. Write the right words.

those   these   feathers   bees

a)

What are _those_?

They're _bees_ .

b)

What are _these_?

They're _feathers_

16

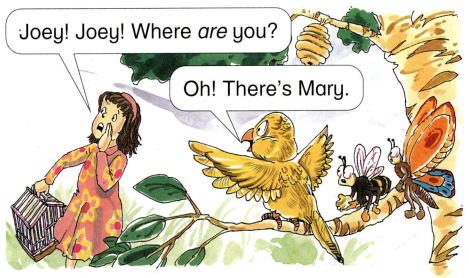

Joey can see Mary. Mary is carrying Joey's cage.
She is looking for Joey.

honey

carrying

looking for

Joey stands on Mary's hand.

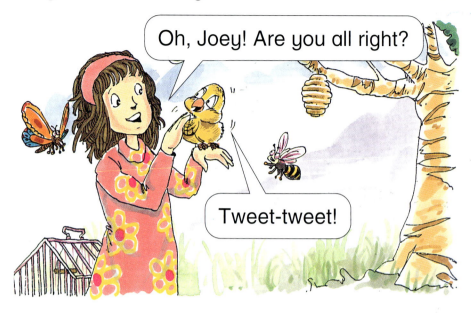

Here's some water and some seeds for you, Joey!

Joey is in his cage. He is happy.
He can see his friends every day.

Questions

Page 1 a) Mary gives Joey some _seeds_ and some _water_.
b) Joey likes the _seeds_ and the _water_.
c) Joey's house is a _cage_.

Page 2 a) Is Joey's cage dirty? _yes Joey cage is dirty_
b) What is Mary doing? _Mary clean Joey cage_
c) What can Joey see? _Joey can se ca brown birds_
d) What are the birds doing? _the brown birds are singing_

Page 3 a) Is it hot? _yes it is hot_
b) Who opens the window? _Mary opens the window_
c) What is Joey doing? _Joey Flies out and stands on Mary's shoulder_

Page 5 a) What colour is Joey? _yellow_
b) What colour are the birds? _brown_
c) What can Joey do? _Jump and Fly_
d) The brown birds live in a _nest_.

Page 6 a) What are the brown birds eating? _worms_
b) Is Joey hungry? _yes Joey is hungry_
c) Does Joey like worms?

Page 7 a) What is behind the tree? _cat_
b) Is the cat hungry? _yes the cat is hungry_
c) Are the brown birds afraid? _yes, the brown birds are afraid_

Page 9   a) Does Joey like cats? No, Joey Does n't *likes eat*
          b) What is the cat doing? *loking at Joey*

Page 10 *True* or *false*?
          a) It is raining. ✓
          b) Joey is dry. ✗
          c) Joey is cold and hungry. ✓

Page 11 a) Is the sun shining? *yes, The sun is shining*
          b) Is Joey happy? *yes, Joey is happy*
          c) What can Joey see? *Joey can see brown birds*

Page 13 *True* or *false*?
          a) Joey can see some flowers and some
              butterflies. ✓
          b) Joey says, ' I like your feathers!' ✓

Page 14 a) Joey stands on a **tree/leaf/flower**.
          b) A **worm/bee/cat** flies out from the
              flower.

Page 15 a) Is the bee angry?
          b) The bee's house is a *beehive*.

Page 17 a) The bee gives Joey some *honey*.
          b) What does Joey like? *Joey I kes eedsand*
          c) What is Mary carrying?

Page 18 a) Is Joey happy? *yes, Joey is happy*
          b) What can Joey see every day? *Joey can see his friend*